Age

Kid's Ukulele Course 2

The Easiest Ukulele Method Ever!

Ron Manus • L. C. Harnsberger

Special thanks to our families, friends, and especially Jennifer, Genevieve, Patrese, and Catherine Harnsberger.

Alfred Music Publishing Co., Inc.
P.O. Box 10003
Van Nuys, CA 91410-0003
alfred.com

ISBN-10: 0-7390-8605-7 (Book & CD)
ISBN-13: 978-0-7390-8605-6 (Book & CD)

Cover and interior illustrations by Jeff Shelly.
Ukulele photo courtesy of Martin Guitars.

 Alfred Cares. Contents printed on 100% recycled paper.

Contents

Tracks 1 & 2

Tuning Your Ukulele

The CD contains all the warm-ups and tunes in Book 2, so you may listen and play along with them. You need to be sure your ukulele is in tune every time you start to play, especially when you want to play along with the CD. Listen carefully to the instructions on Track 1, then use Track 2 to get your ukulele in tune.

Choosing a Ukulele to Use with This Book

It may have been a while since you first started Book 1 of *Alfred's Kid's Ukulele Course*. Since you may have grown a bit or you might want a ukulele with a different sound, you will want to review the sizes and sounds of ukuleles that are available.

Ukuleles come in different types and sizes. There are four basic sizes: soprano, concert, tenor, and baritone. The smallest is the soprano, and they get gradually bigger with the baritone being the largest.

Soprano **Concert** **Tenor** **Baritone**

Soprano, concert, and tenor ukes are all tuned to the same notes but the baritone is tuned to different notes. Each uke has a different sound. The soprano has a light, soft sound, which is what you expect when you hear a ukulele. The larger the instrument, the deeper the sound is. Some tenor ukuleles have six or even eight strings.

The soprano ukulele is the most common, but you can use the soprano, concert, or four-string tenor ukulele with this book. Because the baritone uke is tuned to the same notes as the top four strings of the guitar, you can use *Alfred's Kid's Guitar Method Book 1* to start learning how to play it.

Book I Review

Before starting this book, you need to know all of the following things that were taught in *Alfred's Kid's Ukulele Course,* Book 1. If there's anything you don't remember, go back to Book 1 and review it. Once you are comfortable with all these things, get started with Book 2!

Getting Ready to Play

How to tune your ukulele
How to hold your ukulele
The numbers of your left-hand fingers

How to strum with either a pick or with your fingers
The correct way to place a left-hand finger on a string

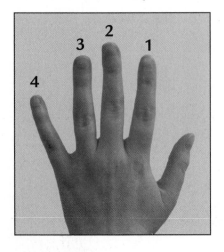

Chords

How to read chord diagrams

Open Strings

Finger I on the second string at the first fret

Finger 2 on the fourth string at the seond fret

1st fret
2nd fret
3rd fret

Strum

The F Chord

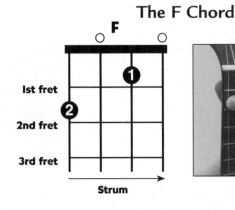

F

1st fret
2nd fret
3rd fret

Strum

The C Chord

C

1st fret
2nd fret
3rd fret

Strum

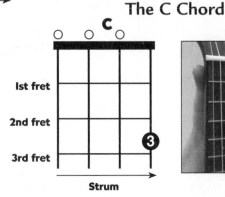

The C7 Chord

C⁷

1st fret
2nd fret
3rd fret

Strum

The G7 Chord

G⁷

1st fret
2nd fret
3rd fret

Strum

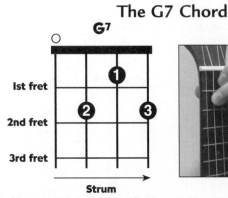

Reading Music Notation

The Staff

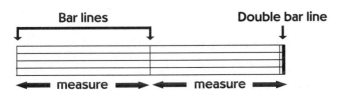

5th LINE
4th LINE
3rd LINE
2nd LINE
1st LINE

4th SPACE
3rd SPACE
2nd SPACE
1st SPACE

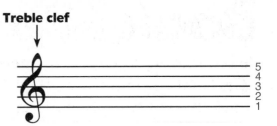

Treble clef

5
4
3
2
1

Bar lines

Double bar line

← measure → ← measure →

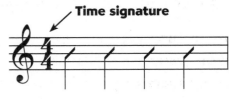

Time signature

Repeat sign	Quarter-note slash	Quarter note	Half note	Whole note	Quarter rest	Half rest

Notes

Notes on the First String: A, B, C

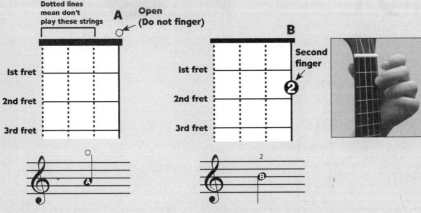

Dotted lines mean don't play these strings

A — Open (Do not finger)

1st fret
2nd fret
3rd fret

B — Second finger ②

1st fret
2nd fret
3rd fret

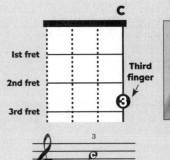

C — Third finger ③

1st fret
2nd fret
3rd fret

Notes on the Second String: E, F, G

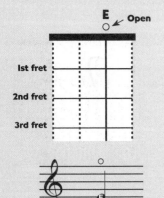

E ← Open

1st fret
2nd fret
3rd fret

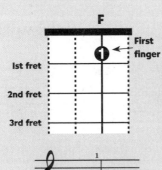

F — First finger ①

1st fret
2nd fret
3rd fret

G — Third finger ③

1st fret
2nd fret
3rd fret

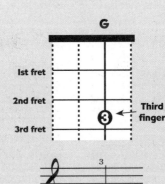 

Notes on the Third String: C, D

C ← Open

D — Second finger ② ← Second finger

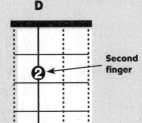 

All the Notes I Know So Far

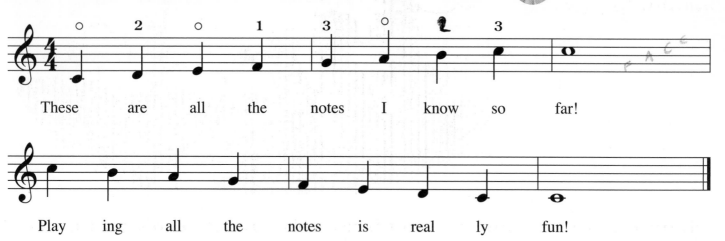

These   are   all   the   notes   I   know   so   far!

Play   ing   all   the   notes   is   real   ly   fun!

Introducing the Octave

When notes have the same name but one sounds higher or lower, the notes are an octave apart. *Octave* means eight (like octopus with eight legs), so two notes with the same name but are eight notes apart are called an octave.

This Is an Octave

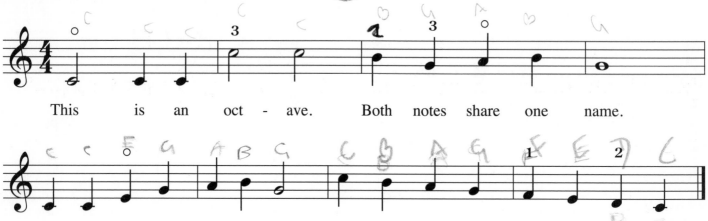

This   is   an   oct - ave.   Both   notes   share   one   name.

They   are   just   eight   notes   a - part.   One,   two,   three,   four,   five,   six,   seven,   eight!

6

Largo

This version of composer Antonin Dvořák's famous melody uses all the notes you know so far except one. Which note is missing?

Largo Track 5

(from the *New World Symphony*)

Antonin Dvořák

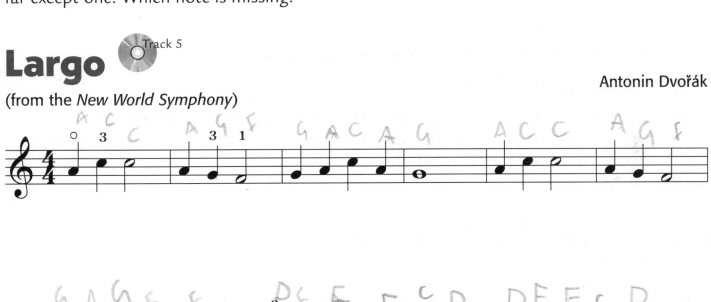

Answer: B

Dotted Half Notes & $\frac{3}{4}$ Time

Introducing the Dotted Half Note

3 beats

This note looks like a half note, but with a dot to the right of the notehead. It lasts three beats.

The $\frac{3}{4}$ Time Signature

A $\frac{3}{4}$ time signature ("three-four time") means there are 3 equal beats in every measure.

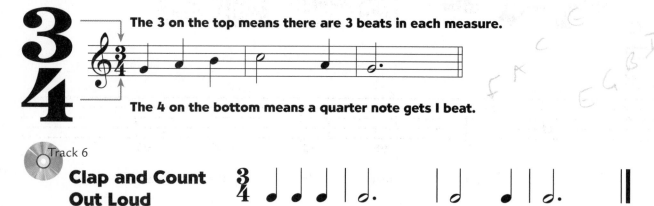

3 The 3 on the top means there are 3 beats in each measure.

4 The 4 on the bottom means a quarter note gets 1 beat.

Track 6

Clap and Count Out Loud

$\frac{3}{4}$

Count: 1 2 3 1 2 3 1 2 3 1 2 3

Three Is for Me!

Track 7

One, two, three. One, two, three. Three is for me!

Play - ing in three with the great - est of ease.

8

The Farmer in the Dell

Track 8

C

The far - mer in the dell,

C

the far - mer in the dell.

C

Hi! Ho! The dai - ry -

C

o, the far - mer in the dell.

9

Beautiful Brown Eyes

Track 9

Beau - ti - ful, beau - ti - ful brown eyes,

smil - ing right in - to my heart. But now

where are those beau - ti - ful brown eyes? Why

must we be so far a - part?_____

Introducing Common Time **C**

This symbol is a time signature that means the same as $\frac{4}{4}$.

C = $\frac{4}{4}$ The 4 on the top means there are 4 beats in each measure.
The 4 on the bottom means a quarter note gets 1 beat.

Old MacDonald
Had a Farm Track 10

Old Mac - Don - ald   had   a   farm,   E - I - E - I - O!   And

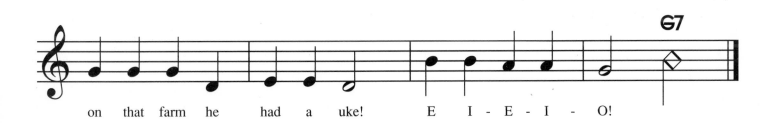

on   that   farm   he   had   a   uke!   E   I - E - I - O!

11

Introducing B-flat

A *flat* ♭ lowers a note a *half step* (the distance from one fret to another is called a half step). B♭ is played one fret lower than the note B. When a flat note appears in a measure, it is still flat until the end of that measure.

Hear this note!
Track 11

1st FRET

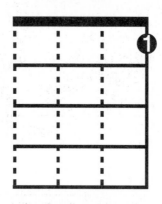

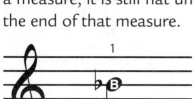

Aura Lee

Track 12

Elvis Presley recorded this folk song as a pop ballad called "Love Me Tender."

New Note B♭

Three-String Boogie

Track 13

This song uses all the
notes you have learned.
Don't forget to listen to
the audio recording first!

Tempo Signs

A *tempo sign* tells you how fast to play the music.
Below are the three most common tempo signs.

Andante ("ahn-DAHN-teh") **slow**

Moderato ("moh-deh-RAH-toh") **moderately**

Allegro ("ah-LAY-groh") **fast**

Three-Tempo Rock

Play three times: first time **Andante**, second time **Moderato**, third time **Allegro**.

Andante Track 14   **Moderato** Track 15   **Allegro** Track 16

Count: 1   2   3   (rest)

14

Rockin' Uke

15

Good Night Ladies

 Track 18
Vocals & Chords

 Track 19
Chords Only

For this song and most of the rest of the songs in this book, you can play either the melody or chords. Your teacher can play the part you aren't playing, or you can play along with the recording.

Moderato

Good   night,   la - dies,   Good   night,   la - dies,

Good   night,   la - dies,   We're   going   to   leave   you   now.

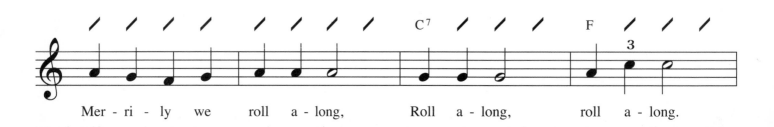

Mer - ri - ly   we   roll   a - long,   Roll   a - long,   roll   a - long.

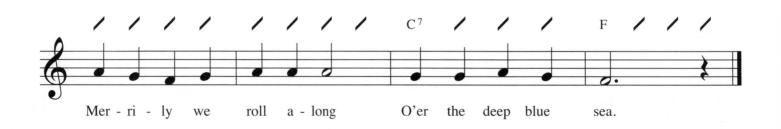

Mer - ri - ly   we   roll   a - long   O'er   the   deep   blue   sea.

Blues in C

Ties

A *tie* is a curved line that connects two of the same note. When two notes are tied, don't play the second note, but keep the first note playing until the second note is done. You are really adding the two notes together.

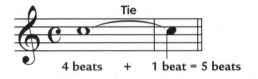

4 beats + 1 beat = 5 beats

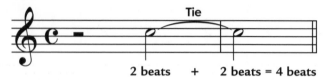

2 beats + 2 beats = 4 beats

Clap and Count Out Loud  Track 21

Count: 1 2 3 4 1 2 3 4 1 2 3 4 1 2 3 4

Down in the Valley  Track 22 Vocals & Chords   Track 23 Chords Only

Down in the val - ley, val - ley so

low, Hang you head o -

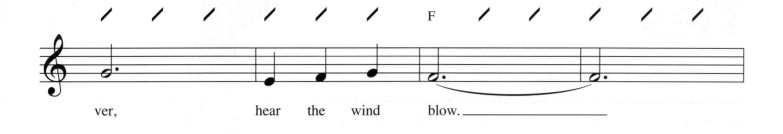

ver,   hear   the   wind   blow._____

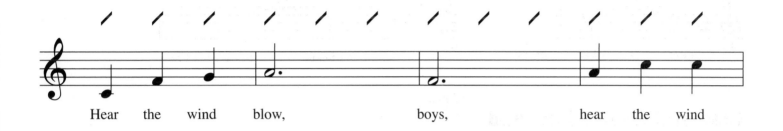

Hear   the   wind   blow,   boys,   hear   the   wind

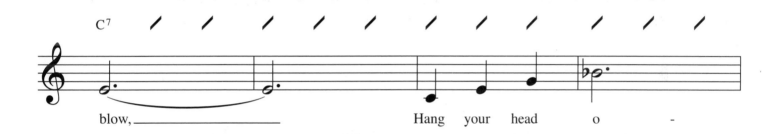

blow,_____   Hang   your   head   o   -

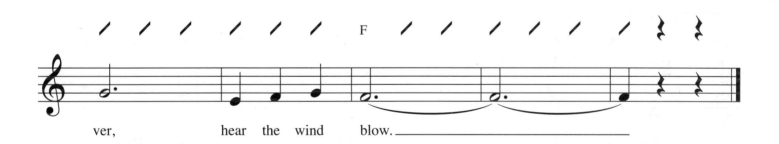

ver,   hear   the   wind   blow._____

Key Signatures

The *key signature* at the beginning of a piece tells you when a note is played as a flat note throughout the piece. In "Ode to Joy," each B is played as B-flat.

Ode to Joy (Extended Version)

Track 24
Vocals & Chords

Track 25
Chords Only

Key Signature: remember to play each B one half step lower.

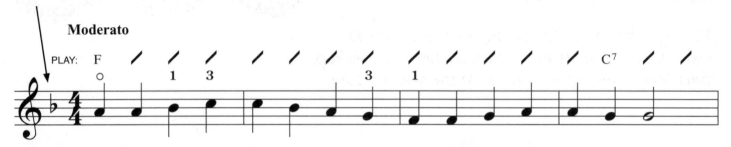

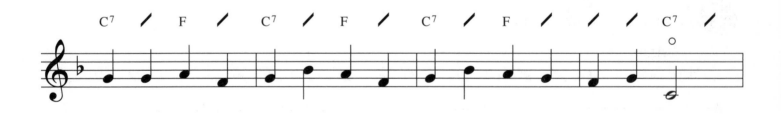

Pickup Measures

Not all pieces of music begin on the first beat. Sometimes music begins with just part of a measure, which is called a *pickup*.

A pickup is like a pumpkin pie. If you were to cut the pie into four equal pieces and take one piece away, there would be three pieces left. If you are playing in 4/4 time and the pickup measure has one quarter note, there will be three quarter notes in the last measure.

Playing in 3/4 time is like cutting the pie into three equal pieces: if there is one quarter note as a pickup, there will be two quarter notes in the last measure.

Clap and Count Out Loud 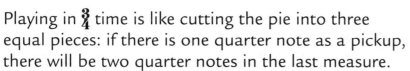 Track 26

Count: (1 2 3) 4   1 2 3 4   1 2 3 4   1 2 3 4   1 2 3 (4)

A-Tisket, A-Tasket

Track 27
Vocals & Chords

Track 28
Chords Only

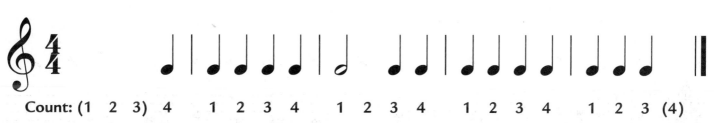

21

Tom Dooley

 Track 29
Vocals & Chords

 Track 30
Chords Only

Moderately slow

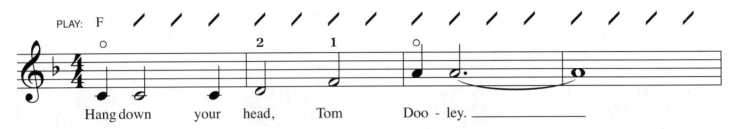

Hang down your head, Tom Doo - ley. _____

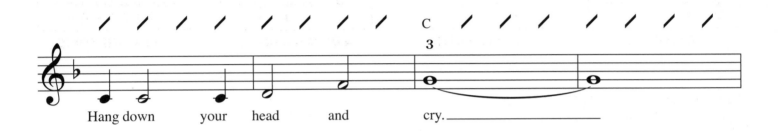

Hang down your head and cry. _____

Hang down your head, Tom Doo - ley. _____

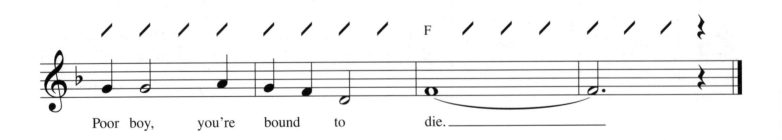

Poor boy, you're bound to die. _____

22

Eighth Notes

Eighth notes are black notes with a flag added to the stem: ♪ or ♩.
Two or more eighth notes are written with beams: ♫ or ♫, ♫♫ or ♫♫.
Each eighth note receives one half beat.

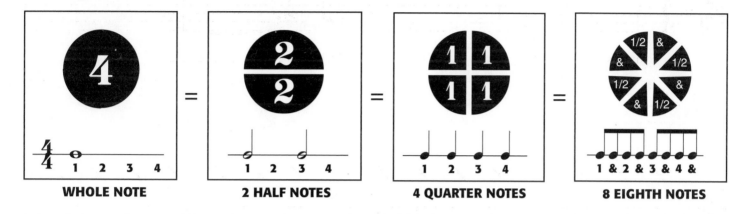

| WHOLE NOTE | 2 HALF NOTES | 4 QUARTER NOTES | 8 EIGHTH NOTES |

Use alternating downstrokes ⊓ and upstrokes ∨ on eighth notes.

Track 31

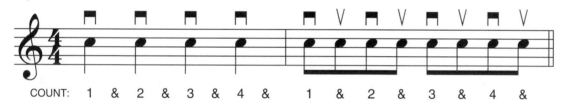

COUNT: 1   &   2   &   3   &   4   &   1   &   2   &   3   &   4   &

Jammin' with Eighth Notes

 Track 32
Melody & Chords

 Track 33
Chords Only

Allegro moderato*

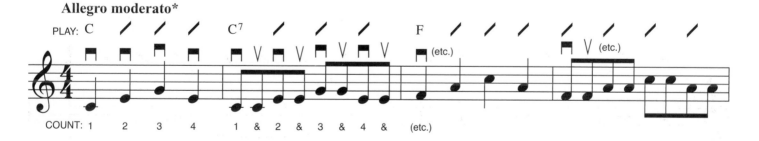

COUNT: 1   2   3   4   1 & 2 & 3 & 4 &   (etc.)

*Allegro moderato means moderately fast.

Go Tell Aunt Rhody

 Track 34
Vocals & Chords

 Track 35
Chords Only

Moderato

PLAY: F   C⁷   F

Go   tell   Aunt   Rho - dy,   go   tell   Aunt   Rho - dy,

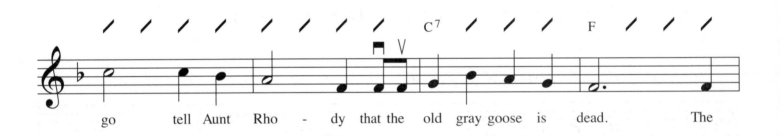

go   tell   Aunt   Rho - dy   that   the   old   gray   goose   is   dead.   The

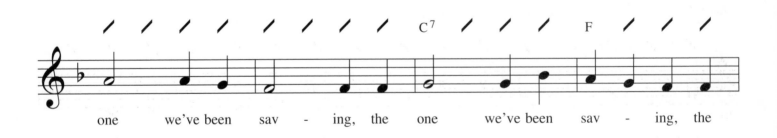

one   we've been   sav - ing,   the   one   we've been   sav - ing,   the

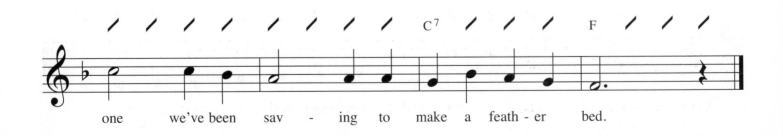

one   we've been   sav - ing   to   make   a   feath - er   bed.

24

Love Somebody (Extended Version)

Track 36
Vocals & Chords

Track 37
Chords Only

Moderately

Love some - bod - y, yes, I do; Love some - bod - y, yes, I do;

Love some - bod - y, yes, I do; Love some - bod - y, but I won't tell who.

Love some - bod - y, yes, I do; Love some - bod - y, yes, I do;

Love some - bod - y, yes, I do; And I hope some - bod - y loves me too.

Clementine

Track 38
Vocals & Chords

Track 39
Chords Only

Moderately fast

In a cav - ern, in a can - yon, ex - ca - vat - ing for a

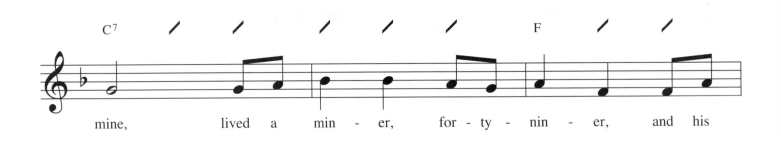

mine, lived a min - er, for - ty - nin - er, and his

daugh - ter, Clem - en - tine. Oh my dar - lin', oh my

dar - lin', oh my dar - lin', Clem - en - tine, you are

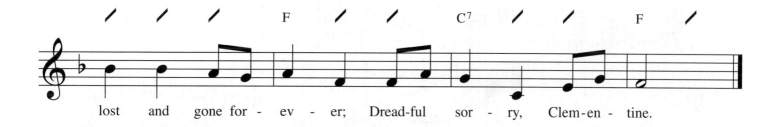

lost and gone for - ev - er; Dread-ful sor - ry, Clem-en - tine.

Additional Verses

Verse 2:
Light she was and like a fairy,
And her shoes were number nine,
Herring boxes, without topses,
Sandals were for Clementine.

Chorus:
Oh my darlin', oh my darlin',
Oh my darlin' Clementine!
You art lost and gone forever
Dreadful sorry, Clementine.

Verse 3:
Drove she ducklings to the water
Every morning just at nine,
Hit her foot against a splinter,
Fell into the foaming brine.

Chorus:
Oh my darlin', oh my darlin',
Oh my darlin' Clementine!
You art lost and gone forever
Dreadful sorry, Clementine.

Verse 4:
Ruby lips above the water,
Blowing bubbles soft and fine,
But, alas, I was no swimmer,
So I lost my Clementine.

Chorus:
Oh my darlin', oh my darlin',
Oh my darlin' Clementine!
You art lost and gone forever
Dreadful sorry, Clementine.

Dotted Quarter Notes

**A DOT INCREASES
THE LENGTH OF A NOTE
BY ONE HALF**

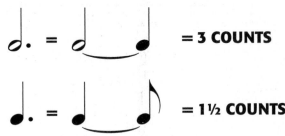

Counting Dotted Quarter Notes

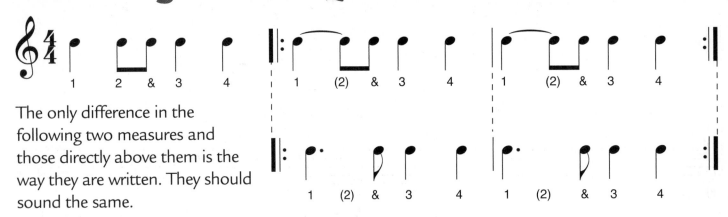

The only difference in the following two measures and those directly above them is the way they are written. They should sound the same.

Cockles and Mussels

 Track 40
Vocals & Chords

 Track 41
Chords Only

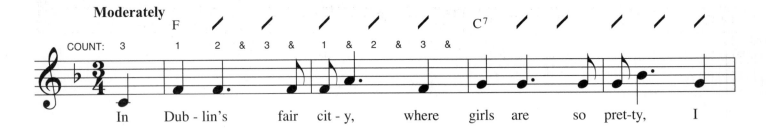

In Dub-lin's fair cit-y, where girls are so pret-ty, I

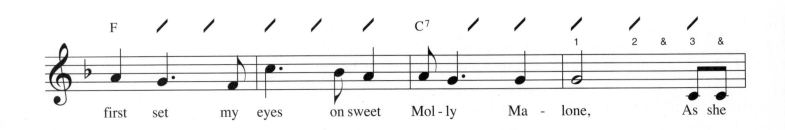

first set my eyes on sweet Mol-ly Ma-lone, As she

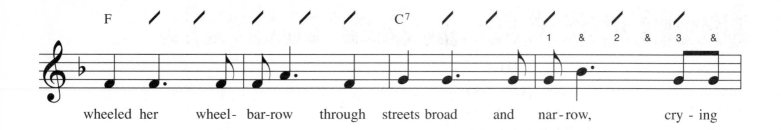

wheeled her   wheel- bar-row   through streets broad and nar-row,   cry - ing

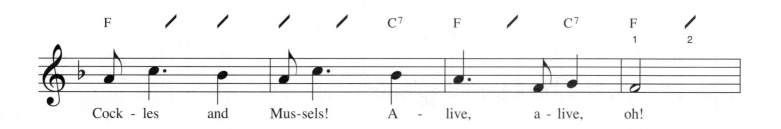

Cock - les   and   Mus-sels!   A - live,   a - live,   oh!

A - live,   a - live,   oh! __   A - live,   al - live,   oh! __   Cry-ing

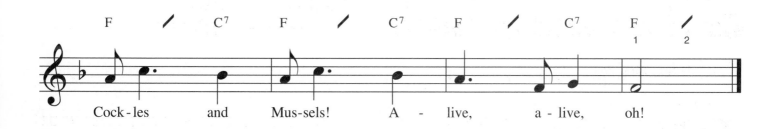

Cock - les   and   Mus-sels!   A - live,   a - live,   oh!

Dynamics

Symbols that show how loud or soft to play are called *dynamics*. These symbols come from Italian words. Four of the most common dynamics are shown here.

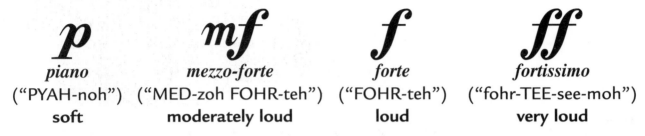

p	mf	f	ff
piano	*mezzo-forte*	*forte*	*fortissimo*
("PYAH-noh")	("MED-zoh FOHR-teh")	("FOHR-teh")	("fohr-TEE-see-moh")
soft	**moderately loud**	**loud**	**very loud**

Echo Rock
Track 42 Melody & Chords • Track 43 Chords Only

The Streets of Laredo

 Track 44
Vocals & Chords

 Track 45
Chords Only

Moderately

PLAY:

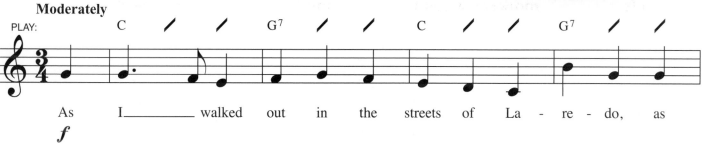

As I_____ walked out in the streets of La - re - do, as

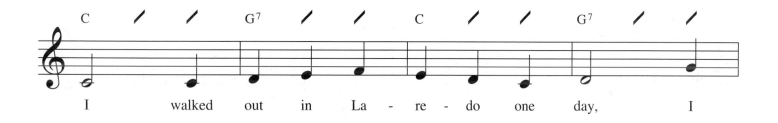

I walked out in La - re - do one day, I

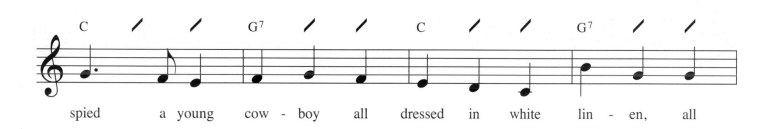

spied a young cow - boy all dressed in white lin - en, all

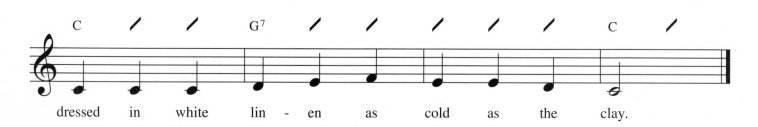

dressed in white lin - en as cold as the clay.

31

The Down-and-Up Stroke Track 46

You can make your accompaniment of waltz songs in $\frac{3}{4}$ like "The Streets of Laredo" more interesting by replacing the second beat of the measure with a downstroke followed by an upstroke. The symbol for downstroke is ⊓; an upstroke uses the symbol ⋁. Together, the down-and-up strokes are two eighth notes that are played in the same time as single quarter note.

Try the following exercise to first just work on the new rhythm.

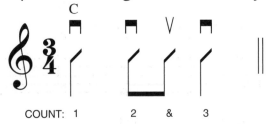

Now practice changing from C to G7.

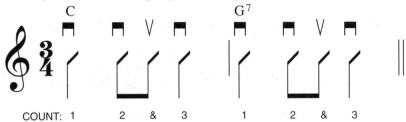

Now practice changing back and forth from C to G7 and back. When you can do it smoothly, go back to page 31 and use it to accompany "The Streets of Laredo."

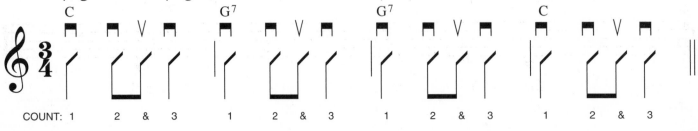

In $\frac{4}{4}$ time, use the pattern ⊓ ⊓⋁ ⊓ ⊓⋁ .

The Fermata

This sign is called a *fermata*. It means to hold the note it is over a little longer.

Michael, Row the Boat Ashore

Track 47
Vocals & Chords

Track 48
Chords only

Moderately slow and steady

Mi - chael, row the boat a - shore, hal - le -

mf

lu - jah! Mi - chael, row the boat a -

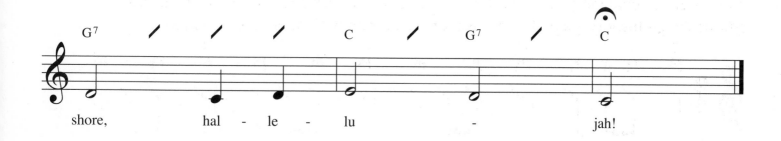

shore, hal - le - lu - jah!

Introducing F-sharp

A *sharp* ♯ raises a note a half step. F♯ is played one fret higher than the note F. When a sharp note appears in a measure, it is still sharp until the end of that measure.

Hear this note!
Track 49

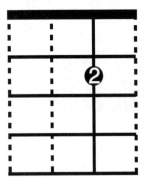

Little Brown Jug

Track 50
Vocals & Chords

Track 51
Chords Only

Brightly

PLAY: G / / / C / / / D⁷ / / /

My wife and I live all a-lone in a lit-tle brown hut we

call our own; she loves gin, and I love rum, I

tell you what, don't we have fun? Ha, ha, ha, you and me,

lit-tle brown jug, don't I love thee? Ha, ha, ha,

you and me, lit-tle brown jug, don't I love thee?

34

The G Chord

Hear this chord! Track 52

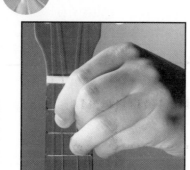

Place your 1st, 2nd, and 3rd fingers in position, then play one string at a time.

Play all four strings together:

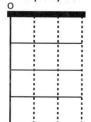 + 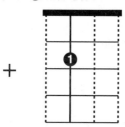 + 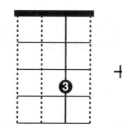 + 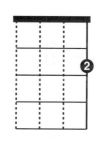 =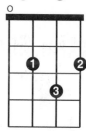

G Chord

The D7 Chord

Hear this chord! Track 53

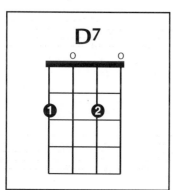
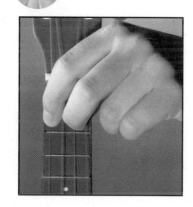

Place your 1st and 2nd fingers in position, then play one string at a time.

Play all four strings together:

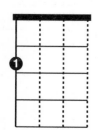 + 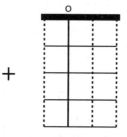 + 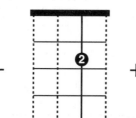 + 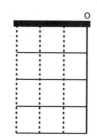 =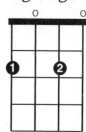

D7 Chord

Over the Rainbow (Extended Version)

The greatest ukulele version of this song was recorded in 1993 by legendary Hawaiian uke player and singer Iz.

Words by E. Y. Harburg
Music by Harold Arlen

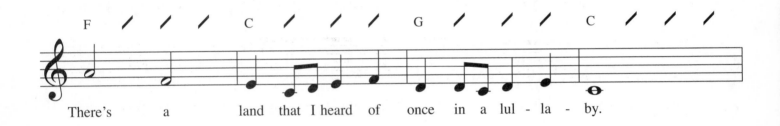

day I'll wish up-on a star and wake up where the clouds are far be-hind me._____ Where

trou-bles melt like lem-on drops, a - way a - bove the chim-ney tops that's where you'll find me.

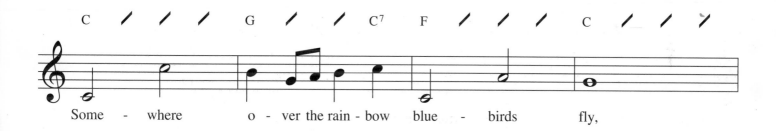

Some - where o - ver the rain - bow blue - birds fly,

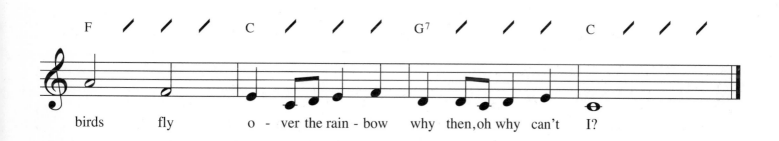

birds fly o - ver the rain - bow why then, oh why can't I?

Review: Music Matching Games

Chords

Draw a line to match each chord frame on the left to the correct photo on the right.

1.
2.
3.
4.
5.
6.

Symbols

Draw a line to match each symbol on the left to its name on the right.

1. | Dotted half note
2. $\frac{3}{4}$ | Whole rest
3. | Tie
4. *ff* | Three beats in a measure
5. | Fermata
6. *Moderato* | Common time
7. *mf* | Loud
8. 𝄴 | Moderately Loud
9. *Allegro* | Soft
10. *p* | Very loud
11. *Andante* | Slow
12. | Moderately
13. *f* | Fast

Notes

Draw a line to match each note on the left to its correct music notation on the right.

1.
2.
3.
4.
5.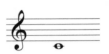
6.
7.
8.
9.
10.

Answer Key

Chords
1: page 4; 2: page 4; 3: page 4; 4: page 4,
5: page 35; 6: page 35

Symbols
1: page 18; 2: page 8; 3: page 8; 4: page 30;
5: page 5; 6: page 14; 7: page 30; 8: page 11;
9: page 14; 10: page 30; 11: page 14;
12: page 33; 13: page 30

Notes
1: page 5; 2: page 5; 3: page 5; 4: page 5;
5: page 5; 6: page 5; 7: page 5; 8: page 5;
9: page 12; 10: page 34;

Ukulele Fingerboard Chart
Frets 1–12

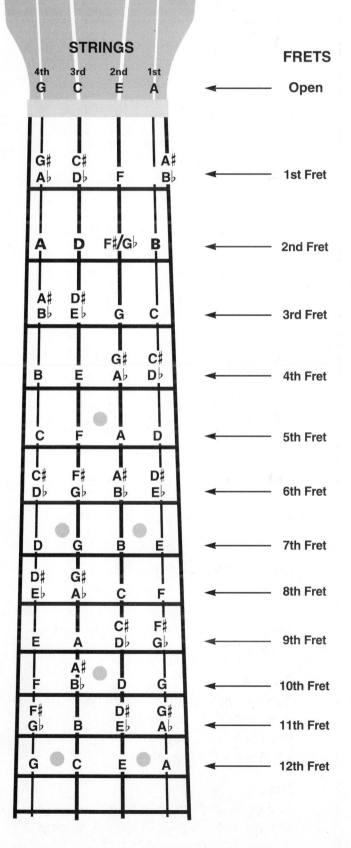

STRINGS				FRETS
4th	3rd	2nd	1st	
G	C	E	A	← Open
G#/A♭	C#/D♭	F	A#/B♭	← 1st Fret
A	D	F#/G♭	B	← 2nd Fret
A#/B♭	D#/E♭	G	C	← 3rd Fret
B	E	G#/A♭	C#/D♭	← 4th Fret
C	F	A	D	← 5th Fret
C#/D♭	F#/G♭	A#/B♭	D#/E♭	← 6th Fret
D	G	B	E	← 7th Fret
D#/E♭	G#/A♭	C	F	← 8th Fret
E	A	C#/D♭	F#/G♭	← 9th Fret
F	A#/B♭	D	G	← 10th Fret
F#/G♭	B	D#/E♭	G#/A♭	← 11th Fret
G	C	E	A	← 12th Fret

Certificate of Completion

This certifies that

_____

has mastered and perfected

Book 2 of Alfred's Kid's Ukulele Course.

_____
Teacher / Parent

_____
Date